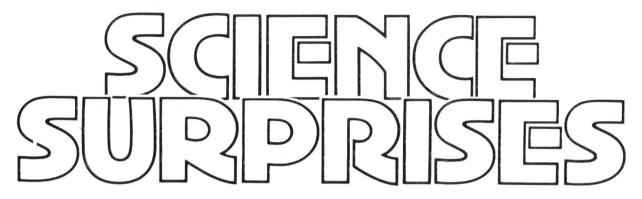

SCIENCE SURPRISES

Gaby Waters

Designed and illustrated by
Graham Round

Contents

Science consultant: Julie Fitzpatrick

About this book

This section contains lots of fun science experiments for you to try.

Some of them are noisy and several are quite messy. There are even some experiments to eat and drink. They all produce surprising and unexpected results.

Meet the monster gang

Each experiment has been tried and tested by the monster gang. They will guide you through each one, step by step.

You can meet the main members of the gang who appear in this book, on the right.

Micky MacMonster, the leader of the monster gang.

Clutty Putty. She is very fond of messy experiments.

Cloth Ears. He is more sneaky than he looks, so watch out.

1

On page 30 there are some extra, more detailed explanations.

As you do each experiment, you can find out how and why it works. You can also discover the science behind all sorts of everyday things.

2

The experiments are completely safe and use ordinary ingredients that you can find at home.

3

Cardboard tubes

Plastic containers

Jam jars

Empty bottles

It's a good idea to start collecting a science equipment kit. Here are some ideas for useful things to look out for.

Normus Noze   Snivel   Parsifal P. Brain

Horace Hogwash, called Hogwash for short.

Slimy Sid and his Aunty Mabel from Australia.

There are lots of other monsters as well.

The Gruesome twins, Fester and Blot

Making frosty patterns

Surprise your friends by covering your bedroom window with these frosty patterns. They look like real frost, but you can even make them on a boiling hot day.

Hogwash is holding the list of things you need. Find out how to make the frost below.

THINGS YOU NEED

MIXING BOWL
SPONGE
CUP
SPOON
WASHING SODA *
HOT WATER (from the tap)

How to make the frost

1 When the crystals disappear they become part of the liquid. In other words, they "dissolve".

Put a cup of washing soda crystals into the bowl, then pour in about the same amount of hot water. Stir them together until most of the crystals disappear.

2 You can wipe the window in any direction, but try not to go over the same bit twice.

Dip the sponge into the liquid and wipe it on to a window. Leave it for about 20 minutes and wait to see what happens.

3 Be careful with food colouring. It can stain things.

To make the frost look icier, add two dessert spoons of blue food colouring to the liquid. Try using other colours as well and see what the frost looks like.

4   *You can buy washing soda in most supermarkets, grocers and hardware stores.

Why the frosty patterns appear

You can wipe the frost off the window with a damp cloth.

As the liquid dries on the window, the water disappears into the air. This leaves the crystals, looking like frost, stuck to the window. The crystals are no longer in big lumps. Now they are spread thinly over the surface of the window.

What is a crystal?

Crystals are solid substances with a regular shape. Lots of things are crystals. Some are shown below.

Sugar

Precious stones such as diamonds and rubies

SALT

SAND

When water contains dissolved crystals it is called a solution.

See if you can find out which of these crystals dissolve in hot water. You can check your results on page 32.

Then try changing them back into crystals by leaving them in a warm place, so the water dries up.

*You can buy Epsom salts in a chemists shop.

Something to try

You can also frost the windows with bath crystals or Epsom salts.* The patterns may be different. Try them and see.

Sea salt crystals

The sea is a solution because it contains dissolved salt. After a swim on a hot day, you sometimes find salt crystals on your skin. The water dries up, leaving the salt behind.

Fizzing and foaming

On these two pages, Micky and the monster gang are mixing ordinary, everyday ingredients to produce fantastic fizzy results. You can do the same. Start with a frothy explosion by making Clutty Putty's bursting bottle.

Things you need

BICARBONATE OF SODA

You may find this in the kitchen, or you can buy it in most supermarkets and chemists.

Funnel

Small jug

Vinegar

Dessert spoon

An empty, litre size plastic bottle and a cork which fits easily into the top.

This bursting bottle makes a monstrous mess, so do it outside.

How to do it

1

Put the bicarbonate of soda into the bottle through the funnel.

Put 4 dessert spoons of bicarbonate of soda into the bottle. Then measure out 10 dessert spoons of vinegar into the jug.

2

The mixture starts fizzing and foaming straight away.

Pour the vinegar into the bottle and quickly push in the cork. Stand well back and wait for the explosion.

How it happens

You can see tiny bubbles of gas in the foam.

When you mix vinegar and bicarbonate of soda they produce a gas, called carbon dioxide. The gas foams and escapes, pushing out the cork with a pop.

6

Other ways of making carbon dioxide gas

ACIDS
DESSERT SPOON OF LIME JUICE
JUICE OF HALF AN ORANGE
JUICE OF 1 LEMON
2 CRUSHED GRAPES

CARBONATES
4 LUMPS OF WASHING SODA
TEASPOON OF BAKING POWDER
SMALL PIECE OF LIMESTONE,
   CHALK OR MARBLE
CRUSHED EGG SHELL

You can mix other things to make carbon dioxide gas. Choose something from each list in this picture and mix them in a jam jar. They will foam and fizz as the carbon dioxide gas escapes.

The ingredients on the left contain a substance called acid. Those on the right are called carbonates. Whenever you mix an acid with a carbonate they make carbon dioxide gas.

Making sherbert fizz

1

MICKY'S SPECIAL SHERBERT MIX
2 SPOONS OF CITRIC ACID CRYSTALS *
1 SPOON OF BICARBONATE OF SODA
6 SPOONS OF ICING SUGAR

2

3

Sherbert powder fizzes because it contains an acid and a carbonate. Try making sherbert yourself by mixing up all the ingredients in Micky's recipe.

Inside Slimy Sid's mouth the citric acid crystals dissolve and mix with the bicarbonate of soda. This produces bubbles of carbon dioxide that make the fizzy feeling.

The bubbles in fizzy drinks are made of carbon dioxide. Make your own drinks fizzy by adding sherbert powder. Put 2 tablespoons of sherbert into each drink.

*You can buy citric acid crystals in a chemists shop.

Wind power

The monster gang are racing their home-made land yachts. The yachts run on wind power, in other words they are pushed by the wind. It's surprising how fast they can move.

Find out how the monsters made their land-yacht below and see if you can improve on their design.

Making a land yacht

1

You may need to cut the polystyrene to the right size.

2

Stick a blob of plasticine on the pointed ends to stop the reels flying off.

Make sure the wheels spin freely. For extra spin, try oiling the needles.

3

Experiment with different shape sails. See which works best.*

For the base you can use a block of polystyrene. This is used for ceiling tiles and packing things. The base of Slimy Sid's yacht is 20cm long and 15cm wide.

For the wheels, thread cotton reels on to both ends of two knitting needles. Attach the needles to the base with sticky tape.

For the mast, push a long stick or knitting needle into the base and secure it with plasticine. Cut out a sail from stiff paper or card. Attach it to the mast and base.

*Clutty Putty has made a square sail. You could try a triangular one, like the sails on real yachts.

The wind at work

As the wind moves, it pushes things around. It is so good at doing this that it is used as a source of power to make things move and work.

The wind fills the sails of boats and wind-surfers and makes them move, just like your land-yacht.

The wind pushes the sails of a windmill round and round. This drives the machine inside the mill.

The yachts work best on a windy day, but you can make your own wind, like this.

Problems with wind power

Now give your yacht a test run. Don't worry if it doesn't sail perfectly at first. You may need to make improvements, especially to the mast and sail.

The problem with wind as a source of power is that it is unreliable. Boats were sometimes stuck on a calm sea with no wind for days and days.

9

Spinning and whirling

Guess what happens when Clutty Putty swings a bucket round and round in the air.

Try it yourself and see. Half fill a small bucket with water then spin it as fast as you can.

The water stays in the bucket.

Do this outside in waterproof clothes, just in case.

Why the water stays in the bucket

As you spin the bucket, the water is pushed outwards. The bottom of the bucket stops the water going any further, so the water sticks to the bottom of the bucket.

Look below to find out more about the force that pushes the water outwards.

Outward force in action

Micky puts ping-pong balls on his monster-disc turntable. The movement of the spinning turntable pushes the balls outwards. There is nothing to stop them, so they fly off.

At the fair

You can see the outward force working at a fairground. Some of the rides that use it are shown

The same outward force holds the rollercoaster to the rails when it loops the loop.

...n this picture. Next time you go the fair, see if you can spot some others.

The outward force pushes you against the wall of this roundabout. It is so strong that you stick to the wall and don't need to hold on.

As the roundabout whirls around, the space rockets are pushed outwards. The rockets are attached to chains to stop them flying away.

Drying things

Spinning and whirling can remove water from wet things and make them dry. A spin-dryer whirls wet clothes round and round in a drum. The water is pushed outwards and escapes through holes in the drum.

In a salad dryer, the salad spins round in a plastic container. The water is pushed out through holes in the container.

How to make Aunty Mabel's salad spinner

Slimy Sid's Aunty Mabel made a salad spinner with an empty slime sorbet tub and a piece of string about 150cm long. You can use any sort of plastic container.

1

Ask someone to help you make holes in the bottom and sides of the tub.

2 Tie knots here to secure the string.

Attach the string to the tub to make a long handle.

3 Do this outside or you won't be very popular.

Put some washed salad in the tub and swing it round and round in the air.

Soapy straw surprises

Have a go at the surprising soapy straw trick below. First find the equipment that the monsters are collecting, on the right.

Like them, you will need a bowl of cold water, 4 matches, a bar of soap and a drinking straw.

1 Float the matches on the water in a star shape, as shown above.

2 Then rub some soap on to the end of the straw.

3 Dip the soapy straw into the water in the centre of the matches. See what happens.

What is happening?

The surface of the water is like a skin. Soap makes a hole in the skin and pushes it away to the edge of the bowl. The matches move with the skin.

You can find out more about water's skin on the opposite page.

Water's skin

The skin on the surface of water is caused by a force called surface tension.

You can see surface tension in action if you fill a cup with water. Do it very gently and you can make the water level rise higher than the cup without it overflowing. Surface tension holds it in place.

Surface tension makes water dripping from a tap form into droplets. Water droplets are firm and round because their skin holds them together.

Droplet squashing game

1

Put some drops of water on a table, just like Micky. Dip a clean straw in water, put your finger over the top and lift it out. Take your finger away and the water will drop out.

2

Now touch the droplets with the soapy straw. See how they spread out and go flat. This happens because soap makes the surface tension weaker and breaks the water's skin.

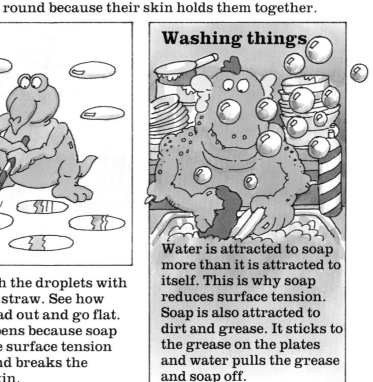

Washing things

Water is attracted to soap more than it is attracted to itself. This is why soap reduces surface tension. Soap is also attracted to dirt and grease. It sticks to the grease on the plates and water pulls the grease and soap off.

13

Tasting tests

In the pictures below, Cloth Ears is doing a tricky taste test on his good friend Normus Noze. Find a trusting friend to help and you can try these taste tests too. Be prepared for some very unexpected results.

Apple or potato?

1

First, Cloth Ears grates some raw apple and potato on to separate plates.

2

Then he gets Normus Noze to block his nose, shut his eyes and open his mouth.

3

Try it yourself. It's really tricky to tell which is which.

He puts a spoonful of apple or potato into Normus Noze's mouth and asks him to guess which it is.

What is happening?

Your tongue can only detect basic tastes. You use your sense of smell to work out the flavours of foods. When your nose is blocked, it is hard to taste the flavour of the food in your mouth.

You card daste dings bery well when you hab a code and your doze iz blockd.

When you take horrid medicine, try holding your nose as you swallow. This should help take the taste away.

Tongue map

Your tongue can detect four basic tastes. These are bitter, sweet, salty and sour. Different parts of the tongue can taste different things.

This picture of Cloth Ears' tongue shows the different taste areas. The areas overlap a bit in most people (and some monsters).

Tongue testing

It tastes sweetest on the tip of my tongue.

Try testing the taste areas of your tongue. Put some sugar in different places on your tongue. Where can you taste it best?

You may not taste bitter things until you swallow as the bitter taste area is at the back.

Do the same with something bitter (strong black coffee), salty (yeast extract or salty water), and sour (vinegar).

Using your eyes

Your eyes also help you taste food. Have a go at the experiments below. You will be surprised how hard it is to taste food when you cannot see it.

Pour out a glass each of grapefruit and orange juice. Blindfold yourself, shuffle the glasses and drink them in turn. Can you tell the difference between them?

Mystery fruit test

1 Cut a bite size chunk out of several different fruits, like the ones in this picture.

2 Blindfold a friend and give him each chunk in turn. Can he tell you which is which?

Static surprises

Micky and the monster gang have discovered some snappy experiments to impress their rivals, the Roughcut Reptiles. Try them out. You will find that strange, almost magic things will happen.

Micky's pool of piranhas

> Give them gaping jaws and sharp teeth so they look like piranha fish.

Cut out 20 to 30 paper fish, each about 3cm long. Put them in a plastic container with a transparent lid.★

Rub a plastic ruler with a woolly scarf quite briskly for about 10 seconds.

Slide the ruler across the lid. Watch the piranha fish jump from the bottom of their "pool" up to the lid.

Sticky surprises

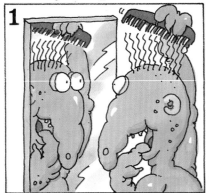

> The monster moves towards the comb as if it is sitting up.

Comb your hair very fast. Hold the comb above your head and look in a mirror to see what happens.

Rub a plastic spoon with a woolly scarf and hold it near a trickle of water. The water bends towards the spoon.

Cut out a tissue paper monster. Rub a plastic ruler on your sleeve and hold it over the monster's head.

★Micky used a mould-flavour mousse container, but you could use an empty margarine tub.

What is happening?

All these experiments happen because of static electricity. Static electricity is not the same as electricity you use at home. You can make it by rubbing things together, as shown below.

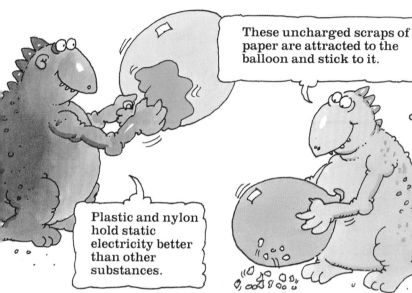

These uncharged scraps of paper are attracted to the balloon and stick to it.

Plastic and nylon hold static electricity better than other substances.

When you rub something it becomes "charged" with static electricity. When something is charged with static electricity, it pulls or "attracts" things that are not charged, like the scraps of paper in this picture.

Crackles and sparks

Clutty Putty is tap dancing in plastic-soled clodhoppers. She rubs her feet on the carpet, then touches a metal radiator. Do this yourself. You may feel a tiny shock of static electricity running through your body.

Feeling static

When you undress, you can sometimes hear crackling noises. If it's dark, you may even see tiny sparks. This is static electricity made by your clothes rubbing together.

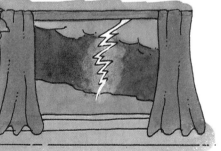

Flashes of lightning are giant sparks of static electricity.

17

Buzzy bee balloon

The buzzy bee balloon whizzes round and round in the air, making a loud buzzing noise. Hogwash and Micky show you how to make it.

How the balloon flies

Scientists describe the way the balloon flies as "action and reaction". This means that movement in one direction causes movement in the opposite direction.

How to make a buzzy bee balloon

1

Long, sausage shape balloons work best.

For the bee's body the monsters use a yellow balloon. Micky draws black stripes all over it and adds two blobs for eyes. Hogwash cuts out tissue paper wings. He makes them quite big so they are the right size when the balloon is blown up.

The buzzing noise is the air rushing out of the balloon.

When you let go of the balloon, the air rushes backwards out of it. This causes a reaction which pushes the balloon forwards.

2

Use tiny bits of sticky tape to attach the wings.

Then they blow up the balloon. Hogwash holds the end tight and Micky sticks on the wings.

3

You can blow up the balloon and make it fly again and again.

Let go of the balloon and watch the bee buzz about. It will whizz around until all the air inside it has gone.

Did you know?

Rockets and jets work in the same way. Hot gases rush out backwards. This pushes them forwards.

18

P. P. Brain's flinging machine

You can see "action and reaction" at work in Parsifal P. Brain's new invention, the flinging machine. You will need a grown-up to help you make it.

You can find these in the middle of a roll of kitchen towel.

THINGS YOU NEED
PLANK OF WOOD ABOUT 20cm LONG
3 NAILS
LONG STRONG RUBBER BAND
STRING
RUBBER BALL
MATCHES
2 CARDBOARD TUBES

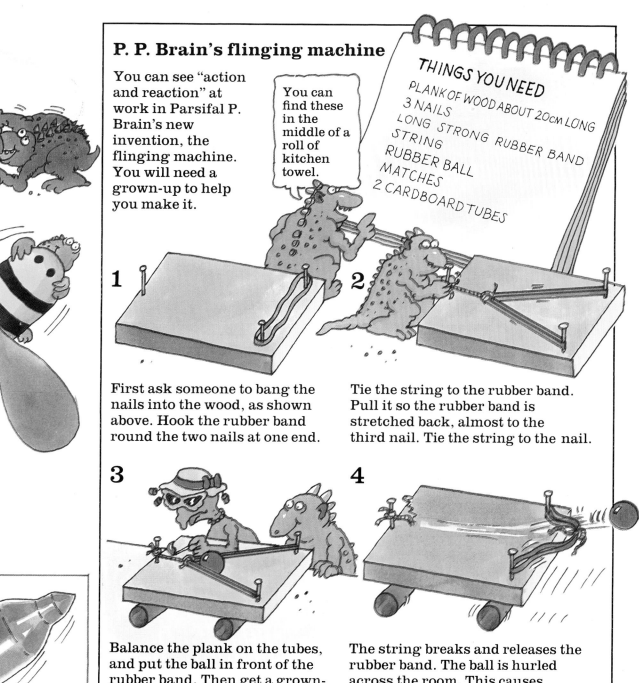

1

First ask someone to bang the nails into the wood, as shown above. Hook the rubber band round the two nails at one end.

2

Tie the string to the rubber band. Pull it so the rubber band is stretched back, almost to the third nail. Tie the string to the nail.

3

Balance the plank on the tubes, and put the ball in front of the rubber band. Then get a grown-up to burn the string with a match. Stand back and watch.

4

The string breaks and releases the rubber band. The ball is hurled across the room. This causes a reaction in the opposite direction and the plank rolls backwards.

Airy surprises

Did you know that air can squash a bottle?

If you don't believe it, try Micky's bottle squashing experiment below.

Micky's amazing bottle squasher

1 Fill the bottle up to about this level.

Pour very hot water from the tap into an empty bottle made of soft plastic.

2 Let the steam shoot out of the bottle and screw the top on quickly. See what happens.

How the bottle is squashed

Air presses down on us all the time. This is called air pressure and it squashes the bottle.

The steam pushes out most of the air.

The air outside presses against the bottle. There is almost no air inside to push against it so it crushes the bottle.

The undrinkable drink

Cloth Ears is preparing a sneaky surprise for his friends.

Press in the plasticine tightly and make sure there are no gaps.

He fills a bottle to the brim with orangeooze and puts a straw in it. Then he pushes plasticine into the bottle neck as a stopper.

Can trick

1

SLIME JUICE

Find a can of fruit juice and make a small hole in it, as Snivel has done.

Try removing the plasticine. The air can get in and you can have a drink.

Now he offers his friends a refreshing slurp. But, however hard they try, they cannot suck up more than a tiny drop. The plasticine stops the air getting into the bottle. You cannot suck up the drink unless there is air pushing down on it to help it up the straw.

Ear-popping

The pressure of the air gets weaker the higher you are.

POP POP

If you gain height quickly, you can sometimes feel your ears popping. This happens because the pressure of the outside air is different from the air in your ears.

You can stop the popping by yawning. This lets outside air into your ears and makes the pressure inside and outside equal.

2

The air pushes up and stops the juice coming out.

Turn the can upside down and see if you can pour out the contents.

3

The air gets in through one hole and pushes the slime out through the other one.

Now make another hole and try pouring out the fruit juice.

Amazing liquids

Clutty Putty's special multi-colour cocktail contains three exotic ingredients in separate layers.

Try making it yourself following Clutty's recipe, below. The ingredients are listed on the right.

INGREDIENTS
FIZZY DRINK
FRUIT SYRUP SUCH AS
BLACKCURRANT CORDIAL
3 TABLESPOONS OF CREAM
COLOURED WITH FOOD DYE

Clutty Putty's cocktail recipe

Don't stir the drink!

Fill a glass with fizzy drink. Clutty Putty's favourite is fizzy melonade. Then pour in enough syrup or cordial to cover the bottom of the glass. Add the coloured cream very gently, one spoon at a time.

Why is the drink in layers?

Density is a word scientists use for comparing weights of different things.

The drink is layered because the ingredients have different weights, or "densities". The syrup sinks to the bottom because it is denser, or heavier than the fizzy drink. Cream is lighter, or less dense, so it stays on the top.

Density test

COOKING OIL
FRUIT CORDIAL
MAPLE SYRUP
MILK
TREACLE
ORANGE JUICE

Can you find out which of these liquids are denser than water and which are less dense? Drop a spoonful of each one into a jar of water and see if it sinks or floats. Check your results on page 32.

Bottle fountain

Now try making a coloured bottle fountain. The Gruesome twins, Fester and Blot, show you how to do it, below.

1

First the twins find two identical bottles. Fester fills one with cold tap water coloured with food dye. Blot and his friend fill the other one with salty water. To make salty water, you mix three tablespoons of salt in a jug of hot water and leave it to cool.

2

3

Fester puts a piece of card over the top of the salty water bottle. He holds the card tight, turns the bottle

upside down and balances it on the other bottle. Blot holds the two bottles and Fester removes the card gently.

The coloured tap water rises because it is less dense than salty water.

You may be able to see some water moving downwards. This is the dense, salty water sinking to the bottom.

Did you know?

Things float more easily in dense (heavy) liquids. This is why it is easier to swim in the sea. The salty water is denser than ordinary water so it helps to keep you afloat.

The Dead Sea in the Middle East is extra salty, so it is very easy to float in it.

Crazy colours

You can make these amazing patterns with your coloured felt pens. The only other things you need are a saucer of water and blotting paper. You can buy this in most stationers shops.

How to make the patterns

1

Write your name on blotting paper using a different coloured felt pen for each letter.

2

Dip the bottom of the paper in the saucer of water. Leave it for a few minutes and watch the patterns appear.

Why the patterns appear

Dark colours, like this, contain more chemicals than others.

Different colours make different patterns.

The inks in your felt pens are made from a mixture of different coloured chemicals. The water rises up the blotting paper taking these chemicals with it.

Different chemicals travel at different speeds and so the colours separate, making patterns. Separating chemicals like this is called chromatography.

Surprising black ink

Black ink is made from lots of different chemicals. These vary with different makes of pen. Try doing some chromatography tests with several different black pens, as Micky is doing below.

1 Label each test strip with pencil so you know which pen made which blob.

Cut several strips of blotting paper and mark each one with a black blob 3cm from the bottom. Use black fountain pen ink and different black felt pens.

2 The colours vary and separate in different ways for each black blob.

Put the strips into a jam jar filled with about 2cm of water. In a few minutes the water separates the different chemicals in each black ink.

3 Shut your eyes tight so you can't see which pen is used.

The monster gang use these chromatography strips for detective work. Slimy Sid writes a mystery message on blotting paper in black pen. Hogwash shuts his eyes.

4 I can tell which pen Slimy Sid used by the way the colours separate.

Hogwash dips the paper in water. When the colours separate, he compares the result with the test strips to find out which pen was used to write the message.

Things to try

You can do chromatography tests on all sorts of things that contain coloured inks or dyes. Some things work better than others. Try them and see.

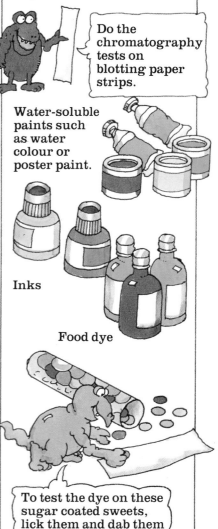

Do the chromatography tests on blotting paper strips.

Water-soluble paints such as water colour or poster paint.

Inks

Food dye

To test the dye on these sugar coated sweets, lick them and dab them on the paper.

25

Sounds surprising

The monster gang are doing some fun experiments with sounds and noises. See what they are doing and try them yourself. Get ready for some strange and surprising sounds.

Spoon Bells

1

Cut a piece of string about a metre long. Then tie it to a small metal spoon as Cloth Ears is doing.

2

3

Hold the ends of the string to your ears. Then ask a friend to tap the spoon on the string with another metal spoon.

The spoons sound like bells and the noise is very loud. Compare the noise they make when you hold the string away from your ears.

Speaking string

The Gruesome twins can talk to each other from the top of the house to the garden with their speaking string. You can do the same. All you need is a length of string with a plastic cup at both ends. Pull the string tight and don't let it touch anything. Whisper into the cup or hold it to your ear to listen.

You can make the string as long as you like, up to about 20 metres.

Attaching the cups

Make a small hole in the bottom of each cup. Push the end of the string through the hole and tie a knot in it.

What is happening?

The spoons sound like loud bells and your voice is heard far away on the speaking string because string is solid.

Sounds travel better and faster through solids and liquids than they do through air.

Hearing games

1

"Don't put the pencil inside your ear."

Put a pencil to your ear and scratch the pencil lightly. The scratching sound travels along the solid pencil. See how loud it sounds.

2

When you go swimming, try making noises or talking to your friends under water. See how different voices and noises sound in water.

3

HISSSSSSS

Just before a train arrives, listen to the rails hissing. The noise of the train travels along the solid rails faster than it does through the air.

Did you know?

Red Indians used to put their ears to the ground to listen for horses in the distance. They could hear the noise of galloping hooves in the ground before they could hear them coming through the air.

27

Come-back can

Micky is showing the monster gang his crazy come-back cans. He rolls them along the ground and they come back on their own, as if by magic. Try making one yourself. You may need some help.

1 Make a hole in the bottom of the container and in the lid. Push the rubber band through the bottom hole and tie a knot at the end.

2 Wrap the stone in cling film and tie it with a piece of string about 15cm long, as shown above.

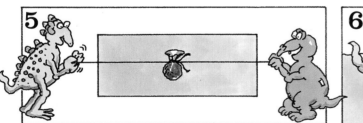

3 Pull the rubber band tight and tie the stone to the rubber band mid-way between each end. You may need help with this.

4 Thread the rubber band through the lid and tie a knot on the outside.

5 The rubber band should be pulled quite tight with the stone in the middle. To make final adjustments, pull the ends of the rubber band and tie new knots.

6 Try rolling your come-back can on a smooth flat surface. If it doesn't roll back, try tightening the rubber band or use a heavier stone.

You can race the cans with your friends.

Crazy rollers

Micky and Clutty Putty have discovered two more crazy can rolling ideas. To try them you will need an empty tin can with a lid.

1. Micky's can

Stick a small lump of plasticine inside the can. Put on the lid and roll it along the floor.

2. Clutty's can

Fill the can with gravel or sand to just below the half-way mark. Push the lid on tight and try rolling it.

How the cans roll

Micky's can

Micky's can wobbles and rolls unevenly. The plasticine lump makes one side of the can heavier than the other.

Clutty's can

Clutty Putty's can hardly rolls at all. The gravel or sand makes the bottom half of the can so heavy that it cannot roll round.

How it works

As the container rolls along the floor, the stone makes the rubber band wind up. When it stops rolling, the rubber band unwinds and the container rolls backwards.

Further explanations

The explanations in this book are obviously highly simplified. The notes below are intended for those who wish to explain the activities in more detail, to older children.

Pages 6-7

These experiments produce a chemical reaction. Acids react with carbonates to give off carbon dioxide (CO_2). They may also produce other substances.

Pages 10-11

The idea of outward and inward forces is used to simplify the explanation of movement in a circle. A more detailed explanation is as follows:

When something moves in a circle, such as a spinning bucket, two forces are at work. The first is the one that makes it move, in other words, the pushing movement of your arm. This obeys the first law of motion which says that an object moves in a straight line unless another force acts upon it.

You can see this law in action if you spin a bucket, then let it go. The bucket flies off. It appears to fly outwards, but if you look closely you will see that it moves in a straight line, at a tangent to the circle of movement. This is what is meant by the simplified term, "outward force" (sometimes referred to as "centrifugal" force).

If you keep hold of the bucket, it does not move in a straight line, but spins round in a circle. This means a second force is acting on the bucket. It is centripetal force, meaning "seeking the centre" and it pulls inwards. When you spin a bucket, your arm is the centrepetal force as it stops the bucket flying away.

Aunty Mabel's salad spinner shows the two forces working very clearly. Your arm and the string handle act as the centripetal force to stop the container flying away. The container does the same thing for the water. Where there are holes in the container, there is no centripetal force to hold in the water. As a result, the water escapes from the container, flying at a tangent to the circle of movement.

Pages 12-13

Surface tension occurs because water molecules attract each other. The molecules at the surface have nothing to attract above them, so they pull extra hard at the sides. This produces a surface layer which acts rather like a skin.

Soap reduces the surface tension of the water by breaking down the forces of attraction between the water molecules. This happens because one end of a soap molecule (the "head") is attracted to water, while the other end (the "tail") repels it.

In the first experiment, the soapy straw breaks down the attraction of the molecules in the centre of the bowl. The molecules at the edge are still strong and so they pull the others towards them. This pulling action plus the pushing of the soap molecules moves the matches. Similarly, when soap touches a firm water droplet, the molecules stop pulling together and spread out.

Soapy water washes dirt away because of the action of the soap molecules. The tail sticks to dirt and grease while the head pulls towards the water. As this happens, the head pulls the tail, bringing the dirt away with it.

Pages 16-17

Everything is made up of tiny particles called atoms. These in turn contain even tinier particles which are charged with static electricity. There are two types: positive charges called protons and negative charges called electrons. Most of the time atoms are neutral or "uncharged" because they have an equal number of electrons and protons.

When two things are rubbed together, electrons sometimes move from one to the other. When this happens the objects are said to be charged with static electricity. The atoms in a charged object have an unequal number of protons and electrons. If there are more protons, it is positively charged. If there are more electrons, it is negatively charged.

Charges of electricity attract charges of the opposite type and repel those of the same type. In these experiments, charged objects attract things that are uncharged. This happens in the following way:

A rubbed balloon is negatively charged. The paper scraps are neutral. The negative charges on the balloon repel the negative charges in the paper, pushing them to the opposite end of the scrap. This leaves the positive charges close to the balloon. It is attracted to them and the paper scraps stick.

These experiments do not introduce the idea of negative and positive charges or repulsion of similar charges.

Pages 18-19

Action and reaction is another way of describing Newton's third law of motion. Newton's law states that for every force that acts, there is an equal and opposite force that reacts.

Pages 20-21

Scientists measure air pressure in millimetres of mercury. At sea level the pressure is 760mm of mercury. Three-quarters of the way up Mount Everest (5 miles above sea level), the pressure is 270mm of mercury.

Pages 26-27

The speed of sound in dry air at normal temperature and pressure is 331.4m (1087.3ft) per second. In sea water it travels at 1540m (5052.5ft) per second.

Results

Page 5: Crystals

Salt and sugar will dissolve in hot water. Sand and precious stones will not.

(If you tried this experiment with precious stones, Slimy Sid would like to know where you found them!)

Page 22: Density test

This chart shows the results for the density test when all the liquids, including the water, are the same temperature.

Fruit cordial Treacle Maple syrup	These sink. They are denser than water.
Cooking oil	This floats. It is less dense than water.
Milk Orange juice	These mix with water. This means they have more or less the same density as water.*

*Milk and orange juice may sink before mixing if they are colder than the water. If they are warmer, they may float before they mix.

Index

First published in 1985 by Usborne Publishing Ltd
20 Garrick Street, London WC2E 9BJ, England.

© 1985 Usborne Publishing Ltd.

The name Usborne and the device ⬥ are Trade Marks of Usborne Publishing Ltd.

Printed in Belgium.